MATERIALS

by Clint Twist

Consultants: Linda McGuigan and Professor Terry Russell
Center for Research in Primary Science and Technology, University of Liverpool

Library of Congress Cataloging-in-Publication Data

Twist, Clint.

Materials / by Clint Twist.

p. cm. — (Check it out!)

Includes index.

ISBN 1-59716-059-8 (library binding) — ISBN 1-59716-096-2 (pbk.)

1. Materials—Juvenile literature. I. Title. II. Series.

TA403.2.T95 2006

620.1'1—dc22

2005009765

For more information, write to Bearport Publishing Company, Inc., 101 Fifth Avenue, Suite 6R, New York, New York 10003. Printed in the United States of America.

1 2 3 4 5 6 7 8 9 10

Contents

Words that appear in **bold** are explained in the glossary.

What Are Materials?

Materials are what things are made of. Different objects are made from different kinds of materials.

Stone, metal, wood, paper, glass, plastic, and cloth are materials. We use them every day.

T-shirt = Cloth

Bottle = Glass

What do you think?

Some things are made
of just one material.

metal

wood

Some things are
made of two or
more different
materials.

Hammer

Which materials are used
to make the hammer?

(Answer on page 20)

5

Stone

Stone is a hard, heavy material.

Stone is dug out of the ground and from the sides of mountains and cliffs.

rough

smooth

Stone = Hard and heavy

Stone can be rough or smooth.

What do you think?

Stone does not bend, but it can be cut into shapes.

These huge stone faces have been cut into the side of a mountain.

Stones in water

Most stones do not **float**. What will happen if you drop stones in water?

(Answer on page 20)

7

Metal

Metal is a material made from some kinds of stone. The stone is smashed into powder. It is then heated to remove the metal.

Iron comes from a stone called hematite.

Metals are strong and difficult to break. They are usually shiny.

Metal = Hard and shiny

What do you think?

Metals are hard like stone, but they can be bent and twisted into different shapes.

Why can metal be used to make this fence?

Metal fence

(Answer on page 20)

Wood

Wood is a material that comes from trees.

Wood floats.

Wood = Floats

What do you think?

Wood is a hard material, but it is not as hard as stone or metal. Wood can be cut and shaped with metal tools.

Wooden violin

Why is wood used to make many boats?

Wooden boat

(Answer on page 20)

Paper

Paper is a soft material that is made from tiny pieces of wood.

Wood pulp

Paper is light and very easy to bend and fold.

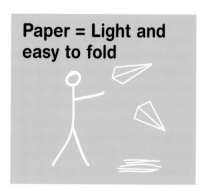

Paper = Light and easy to fold

What do you think?

Chairs are made of hard and strong materials, such as wood or metal.

Paper chair

Why can't chairs be made out of paper?

(Answer on page 21)

Glass

Glass is a hard material that is made from sand. The sand is heated until it is very hot. Then it melts and turns into glass.

Glass is soft when it is hot. It becomes hard when it cools. You can see through most kinds of glass.

Glass = Hard

What do you think?

These glass windows let light in and let the dogs see out.

Some glass bottles

You cannot see a drink inside a metal can. Can you see a drink inside some glass bottles?

(Answer on page 21)

15

Plastic

Plastic is a material that is usually made from **oil**. The oil is pumped out of the ground. It is then heated and mixed with other ingredients to make plastic.

Plastic can be hard or soft. It is light and can be made into any shape or color.

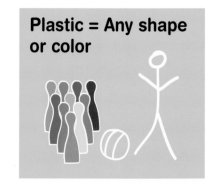

Plastic = Any shape or color

What do you think?

Some plastic is easy to bend. You can even see through some plastic.

Some plastic

Which plastic objects in this picture can you see through?

(Answer on page 21)

Cloth

Cloth is a soft material. There are different kinds of cloth.

Some cloth is made from sheep's wool.

Some cloth is made from a cotton plant.

Sheep's wool = Cloth

Cotton plant = Cloth

What do you think?

Sheep's wool and cotton are spun into **yarn**.
The yarn is woven or knitted into cloth.

The cloth is
used to make
many things,
such as T-shirts
and jeans.

Cloth

You can't fold a piece of wood
or glass. Why can you fold a
piece of cloth?

(Answer on page 21)

19

Answers

Page 5

Wood and metal are used to make the hammer.

Hammer = Wood and metal

Page 7

Most stones will sink to the bottom of the water.

Stones in water = Do not float

Page 9

Metal can be used to make the fence because it can be bent and twisted into different shapes.

Metal fence = Hard and bendable

Page 11

Wood is used to make many boats because wood floats on water.

Wooden boat = Boat floats

Page 13

Paper is not hard or strong enough to be used for making chairs.

Paper chair = Not hard and strong

Page 15

You can see a drink through some glass bottles.

Some glass bottles = See-through

Page 17

You can see through the water bottle, the sunglasses, and the sandwich container.

Some plastic = See-through

Page 19

Cloth is soft so it can be folded.

Cloth = Soft and can be folded

Glossary

cloth (KLOTH)
a kind of material that is made from fibers fastened together by weaving or knitting

float (FLOHT)
to lie on top of water or air

glass (GLASS)
a hard material made from sand

materials (muh-TIHR-ee-uhlz)
any substance from which things are made

metal (MET-uhl)
a hard, strong material, such as gold or iron

oil (OIL) a greasy liquid

paper (PAY-pur)
a lightweight material made from chopped-up wood

plastic (PLASS-tik)
an artificial material that can be made into almost anything

stone (STONE)
a hard material made from minerals that are found in the earth

wood (WUD)
a hard material that makes up the trunk and branches of a tree

yarn (YARN)
a long thread made of fibers twisted together

23

Index

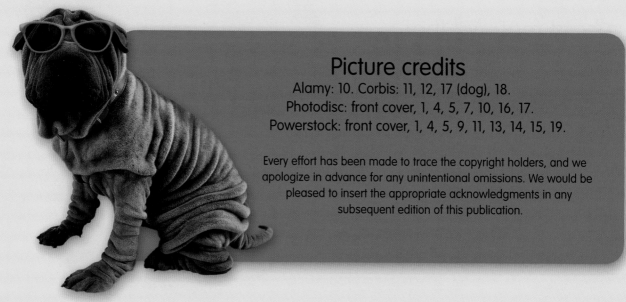

Picture credits

Alamy: 10. Corbis: 11, 12, 17 (dog), 18.
Photodisc: front cover, 1, 4, 5, 7, 10, 16, 17.
Powerstock: front cover, 1, 4, 5, 9, 11, 13, 14, 15, 19.

Every effort has been made to trace the copyright holders, and we apologize in advance for any unintentional omissions. We would be pleased to insert the appropriate acknowledgments in any subsequent edition of this publication.